AUTHOR'S NOTE

*The stories in this book are about real people and real events. In some stories there are
a few imagined characters doing the kinds of things people would have done.*

*Each of the castles in this book can be visited. The Tower of London, Castel Sant'Angelo
and Osaka are crowded museums in the middle of cities. Chambord in the forest
and Neuschwanstein in the mountains are almost unchanged. Caernarfon, Bodiam
and Krak des Chevaliers are partly ruins, Chateau Gaillard more so.
Windsor Castle is still a royal residence.*

For Liz ~ S.B.

To Ben ~ M.H.

Numbers like this ◇ help you find your way around the pictures.
When you come across a number in the story, check where it appears on the small picture.
Then turn back the page to find your place on the big picture.

Stephen Biesty's
Castles

Written by
Meredith Hooper

ENCHANTED LION BOOKS

New York

CONTENTS

This book tells ten stories
about ten amazing real castles.

PAGE
6

CHATEAU GAILLARD

FRANCE ~ OCTOBER 5, 1198

King Richard I of England builds
a glorious new castle to challenge
his old enemy. But how long
will it last in the hands of
his brother?

PAGE
10

KRAK DES CHEVALIERS

SYRIA ~ MARCH 29, 1271

Sultan Baybars
attacks the
mighty castle of
Krak des Chevaliers. Will he win it back from the
crusader Knights who defend it?

PAGE
14

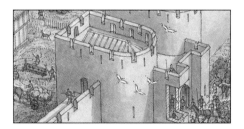

CAERNARFON CASTLE

WALES ~ AUGUST 20, 1320

William the stonemason looks
down from the castle gateway at
the busy streets of Caernarfon.
Could the town be a hiding place
for Welsh spies?

PAGE
18

WINDSOR CASTLE

ENGLAND ~ JANUARY 19, 1344

Edward III, King of
England, holds a magnificent
tournament at Windsor Castle.
What rewards lie ahead for
his loyal knights?

PAGE 22

BODIAM CASTLE
ENGLAND ~ MAY 25, 1392

Sir Edward Dallingridge gets ready for a feast at Bodiam. But who are the mysterious visitors riding towards the castle?

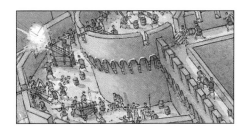

PAGE 26

CASTEL SANT' ANGELO
ITALY ~ MAY 6, 1527

Benvenuto Cellini shoots at the enemy from the top of Castel Sant'Angelo. But how does he end up in one of its dungeons?

PAGE 30

TOWER OF LONDON
ENGLAND ~ MAY 29, 1533

King Henry VIII welcomes his new Queen, Anne Boleyn, to the Tower of London. Why does Anne weep when she returns three years later?

PAGE 34

CHAMBORD
FRANCE ~ DECEMBER 18, 1539

Francis I, King of France, entertains an Emperor at the vast Chateau of Chambord. How far will he go to impress his guest?

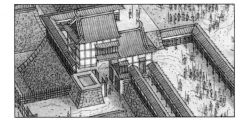

PAGE 38

OSAKA CASTLE
JAPAN ~ NOVEMBER 30, 1614

Young Lord Hideyori prepares to defend Osaka Castle against Ieyasu's huge army. Who will be the victor?

PAGE 42

NEUSCHWANSTEIN
GERMANY ~ FEBRUARY 7, 1886

King Ludwig II dreams about his fairytale castle of Neuschwanstein. Will it bring him the happiness he longs for?

CHATEAU GAILLARD

—

OCTOBER 5, 1198

KING RICHARD I OF ENGLAND IS BUILDING A CASTLE IN NORMANDY, FRANCE. Chateau Gaillard is only three days' hard ride from Paris, the capital city of his bitter rival, the French King Philip Augustus.

The King is here! The message speeds around the castle. ⟶

Pick-men deepening and widening the outer ditch ◇1 hack even harder at the chalk-white rock. Roofers bend their backs and heave the blue slate tiles up the dizzying curve of the forward tower roof ◇2. Cooks stop chattering and stir the cauldrons of soup in the outdoor kitchen ◇3. Carpenters saw even faster through the sweet-smelling timber ◇4. Chips of stone fly, as masons square the heavy blocks of stone ◇5.

A hod-carrier hurries and trips, dropping his load of cement ◇6. Heaven protect him if the King sees. The blacksmiths ◇7 snigger as they sweat over their fires, sharpening pickaxes and chisels. The cement dribbles down the wall.

But King Richard is up on the great keep ◇8. Powerful body braced against the autumn wind, red-gold hair, bold blue eyes. Revelling in the hammering, clattering and clanging – the continuous din of hundreds of men working.

Hubert the master engineer waits respectfully. He needs to discuss the keep's new-fangled fortifications, but the King is busy talking at a bishop just arrived from England.

"Look at my castle! Two years ago there was nothing here. Only a great bend in the river, steep cliffs carved by the yellow current, a scattering of islands. And now – marvel at the greatest castle the world has ever seen.

"I know every stone. I arrive when no one expects me. Push and push again for speed. My heart longs to finish. Ever since I was sixteen, my chin still boy-smooth, I've been fighting up and down the lands of France. Now, all my experience of sieges, of fortification and weapons are concentrated in this one glorious, unbeatable design. Look below, at the

stout walls of the inner ward ◇9. See how they rise sharply from the deep ditch, cunningly curved, like half-skittles, to deflect missiles and send them ricocheting back on to attackers.

"I've spent more on my Chateau Gaillard, my cheeky castle, than on all my castles in England. And why? My castle shouts a challenge to my enemy the King of France, Philip Augustus. I'm building it right on the boundary of my territory. Never forget, my Lord Bishop, that I, Richard the Lionheart, own more land in France than that treacherous Philip Augustus. You know how deeply I hate him. I don't need reasons. But I will remind you.

"Eight years ago, we led our armies all the long way to the Holy Land to fight together in a crusade. Before we left, we signed a treaty to stop fighting each other in France. But, once in the Holy Land, in the heat and toil of battle against the mighty Saladin, Philip Augustus said he had to go home. Back in France, he found excuses to invade my lands. And I! I was captured on my way home and imprisoned in Germany. Cunning Philip Augustus plotted to keep me captive. My English subjects had to pay a King's ransom – thirty-four tons of silver – to get me free.

"I've fought ever since, hard, long years, to claw back my French territories lost to Philip Augustus. I tell you, my Lord Bishop. This new castle of mine is invincible. I could hold it, even if the walls were made of butter."

And King Richard is off down the stairs, master Hubert the engineer running after him.

Next spring, at the start of the campaigning season, King Richard is besieging a small castle south of

Chateau Gaillard. A bold crossbowman up on the ramparts taunts the attackers. He only needs a frying pan to defend himself, he shouts. Richard goes to look. He isn't wearing enough protection. He raises his shield a split second too late, as a shot from the crossbow thuds into his shoulder.

The King has seen enough wounds to know what will happen. Gangrene sets in. On April 6, 1199, Richard I dies, aged 41. "In this man's death," sing sad minstrels, "the lion by the ant was slain."

Richard's brother John becomes King. John finishes building Chateau Gaillard. But he adds a window in the outer wall of the chapel ◆10◆, high above the steep cliffs facing the river, and he adds a toilet, emptying down a chute.

King Philip Augustus has long schemed and fought to uproot the English from France. He would not challenge Chateau Gaillard while Richard was alive. But John is a different matter. In September 1203, the French King lays siege to the castle in a carefully planned campaign. Richard's stockade ◆1◆ across the river is destroyed, his island fort, bridge ◆2◆, and all defences surrounding the castle site are taken. An English attempt to relieve the siege fails.

Chateau Gaillard is screwed into a pincer-tight blockade. Townspeople who took refuge in the castle are pushed out to save food. They lie in the ditches, starving. Catapults continually hurl missiles at the castle walls. Crossbowmen shoot from the top of roughly made wooden towers.

With great difficulty, the outer curtain wall ◆13◆ is mined and breached. Now the attackers face the

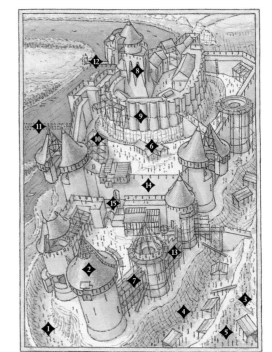

seemingly impregnable middle ward ◆14◆. But a soldier called Bogis has been poking around. He crawls up the cliffs below the chapel wall and wriggles up the slimy toilet drain. With five mates, he climbs through the chapel window, and makes a dreadful racket to sound like a large detachment of invaders. The shocked garrison try to smoke them out. In the confusion, Bogis and his five mates let the drawbridge ◆15◆ down, and the French rush in.

A vast siege engine is hauled up to batter the inner ward. Sappers tunnel under the wall. The defenders are so exhausted they do not even attempt a last stand in the great keep.

On March 4, 1204, after a six month siege, Richard the Lionheart's magnificent fortress of Chateau Gaillard falls.

10

KRAK DES CHEVALIERS

—✦—

MARCH 29, 1271

THE MIGHTY CRUSADER CASTLE OF KRAK DES CHEVALIERS IS UNDER SIEGE. The Knights of St. John have held this Syrian castle for 161 years. Now, Baybars, Sultan of all Egypt, is attacking it.

Miserable villagers crouch inside the castle walls. Missiles crash from the sky. Fire bombs of naphtha shatter and burn. The walls shudder. In the stone chapel, the knights pray. Their massive castle is a magnificent fighting machine, designed to repel invaders, to withstand sieges. It has wells of fresh water, fodder for horses, workshops, a windmill to grind corn.

Two thousand men can be garrisoned here. But reinforcements have a long, hard journey from Europe. Now only sixty knights are defending Krak des Chevaliers, assisted by local troops.

Outside, the powerful army of Baybars, Sultan of Egypt, attacks relentlessly.

Baybars has superb cavalry ◇1, battle-seasoned crossbowmen ◇2 and thousands of footsoldiers ◇3. He has siege engineers, surgeons and preachers, and a huge baggage train. His men are armed with spears, axes, swords, daggers, hand-held slings for hurling stones, bows and arrows. His siege engines ◇4 can aim accurately, hurling heavy rocks further than an arrow can travel, pounding the strongest walls to rubble. Men on both sides give siege engines nicknames. Names like Devilish, or The Evil Neighbor.

Baybars ◇5 is a fierce fighter, an outstanding leader. Tall and strong, brown-skinned, blue-eyed, he was captured as a boy on the south Russian steppes, sold as a slave, converted to Islam and trained to fight in the elite troops of the Sultan of Egypt. The previous Sultan was murdered after returning from a battle. Baybars, deeply involved in the murder, was elected new Sultan.

Now Baybars is fighting to rid the area of European invaders. To Christians, this is the Holy Land. Europeans have fought hard crusades here. But Baybars is determined to capture and destroy the Christians' network of strong, cunningly-defended castles. They are thorns in the flesh of Islam. And Krak des Chevaliers is the greatest, sharpest thorn.

For the first ten days of the siege, rain beating in across the mountains turned the ground to mud, forcing the attackers to wait. Then the weather cleared. The heavy siege engines were hauled into place. The triangular-shaped outer defences ◇6 fell, becoming the new forward position. Baybars stationed crossbowmen amongst the broken walls to pick off defenders. The siege engines were dragged closer.

Krak des Chevaliers is built on a rocky spur of hills. Steep slopes surround and protect it on three sides. At the castle's center is a courtyard ◇7, almost covered in vaulted stone passageways to resist hurling missiles. The only way into the courtyard is up Krak's dreaded Great Ramp ◇8, a long dark tunnel, cut with openings which let in dazzling sunlight. The Ramp doubles back up a hairpin bend, with murder holes, trick routes and multiple gates. The outermost entrance gate can only be reached from the plain below.

But Baybars is attacking from the south side, where the ground rises. Here, the castle's inner line of defence is a massive sloping wall ◇9, with arrow slits reached by a secret passage ◇10. Three high, round towers grow out of the slope, and its base is protected by a deep cistern of water ◇11. Beyond are the towers and wall of the outer line of defence ◇12, completely surrounding the castle.

Baybars has found the weakest point in this outer wall, the south-west tower ◇13. A strong wooden shed on wheels ◇14 has been dragged right up against its foot, like a fat leech. Inside, Baybars' sappers are undermining the tower's foundations.

Baybars is a brilliant general. He leads from the front, checking the sappers' tunnel, shooting with the crossbowmen. Now, on March 29, he gives the signal. With a dreadful rumbling roar, the undermined tower collapses. The waiting troops storm the breach. Drums hammer, trumpets hoot, gongs and cymbals clang – a frightful, thundering din to terrify the people inside. The attackers enter the outer ward. The defenders are slain, the local soldiers from the mountains taken prisoner, the villagers are allowed to go free.

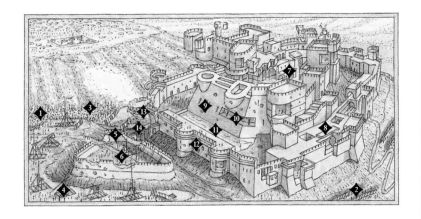

Krak's superb inner defences, where the knights have retreated, are still intact. Baybars does not want to destroy this mighty castle. Open fighting – the sword – should only be used when other methods have failed. Use the dagger for secret attack. Use cunning, deception. Baybars has spies everywhere, and spies who spy on the spies. He is ruthless, clever, he keeps everyone uncertain about what he will do next. Sometimes he tricks even his closest advisers, and isn't where they think he is. He has set up an efficient postal service using horses, camels and carrier pigeons. All letters come to Baybars, so he knows everything that happens, fast.

Now Baybars delivers a letter to the Knights. It seems to come from their Grand Master, the head of the Knights of St. John, giving them permission to surrender. The letter is a forgery. Perhaps the Knights know. But it's their only chance. They surrender on April 8, and Baybars allows them to ride out in safety.

The great castle of Krak is his. He's kept the damage down, and immediately his workmen begin repairs.

Four weeks later, Baybars faces a new threat. Prince Edward of England arrives in the Holy Land with a reinforcement of knights. Baybars arranges a truce for ten years, ten months, ten days and ten hours. Muslims and Christians have always mixed peace with war. But Baybars fears that Edward might return with a bigger army. He orders a member of the tribe of Assassins to work in Edward's private apartment, pretending to be a servant. As the Prince rests, the Assassin stabs him in the stomach with a dagger. Edward fends off the murderer and survives. He returns to England where his father has died. He is now King Edward I.

Five years after taking Krak des Chevaliers, Sultan Baybars is dead. The rumour is whispered that he ordered a cup of fermented mare's milk for an enemy king who drank and died, horribly. By mistake, people say, Baybars drank from the same cup, where enough poison remained to kill him.

13

Caernarfon Castle

— ❧ —

August 20, 1320

The great brooding presence of Caernarfon Castle punches towards the sea like a mailed fist. Begun nearly forty years ago by King Edward I of England, the castle is still unfinished.

William climbs hand over hand up the wooden rungs of the ladders, counting. He's used to working high. Stonemasons have to. But counting's a kind of lucky charm.

Sixty-nine, seventy, seventy-one – then he's arrived, ➤

up with the statue ① of King Edward II above the great gate ② of Caernarfon Castle. Beyond and to either side sprawls the massive castle. William knows all the cunning and elaborate defences. He's explored the winding stairs, fumbled along the narrow passages, peered through all the doors. Stonemasons build walls, then they have to mend them.

William leans around and checks the two iron clamps holding the heavy carved stones of the King's statue. "Mind," his mother used to say, as he worked in the mason's yard ③, coaxing the stone into the image of the King. "Our Edward is a handsome man, and don't you forget it. Born right here in Caernarfon, bless him." And William, bending over his chisel, making the tight curls of the King's beard, the proud stare of his eyes, would remember the story he'd heard all his life. How King Edward I, head and shoulders taller than everyone else, came home from the crusades and conquered Wales. How he built a belt of massive stone castles to tighten his hold over the Welsh. How Queen Eleanor, who travelled wherever the King went, came to Caernarfon Castle, the mightiest of all, to give birth to their baby. The walls were only partly built. But the Queen's baby, her fourteenth, was a strong healthy boy, christened Edward. How the King said his new son, born in Wales, was a Welsh prince.

But the King and Queen never came back to their great royal fortress-palace in Caernarfon. Their rooms waited, empty. The chambers for the princes and princesses, the private chapels for their prayers – all empty.

Now Edward I and Queen Eleanor are both long dead. Their son, the Welsh prince, rules as King Edward II. And he has not come back here, ever, either. Inside the castle, spiders scuttle across the stone-flagged floors. The sea wind whistles at the shutters. Pigeons sidle through the arrow slits and flap along the dark passages ④ in the thickness of the walls. There are only thirty men in the castle garrison. Ten of them are crossbowmen ⑤. The rest are doorkeepers, caretakers, sentinels, a few laborers.

William pulls an apple out of his tunic and sits on his heels, munching. Seagulls hover on the wind. There are more birds in this lonely place than humans. That's certain. William can see his woman down in the town, fetching water from the conduit in the market square ⑥. She'll stop and talk to her brother, the soldier. He's here on a visit, and William can see him showing his longbow to eager boys.

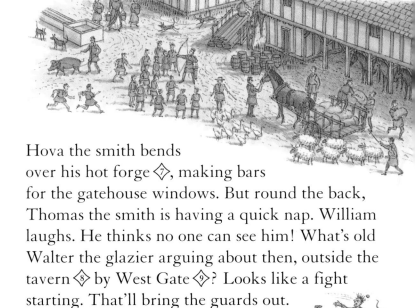

Hova the smith bends over his hot forge ⑦, making bars for the gatehouse windows. But round the back, Thomas the smith is having a quick nap. William laughs. He thinks no one can see him! What's old Walter the glazier arguing about then, outside the tavern ⑧ by West Gate ⑨? Looks like a fight starting. That'll bring the guards out. Mad Nick is in the stocks again.

William looks over to the wharf ⑩. It's busy.

16

Supplies coming in from everywhere, quarried stone, heaps of coal, thick, long lengths of timber for the new hall ◈ being built behind the gatehouse. There's a regular holdup in front of the West Gate. Carts backed up. Always takes so long checking the papers and goods of people entering the town. But the local Welsh have got to come in to trade. Then they've got to leave again, at sunset. The curfew bell rings, and they're out, the gates locked. You can't be too careful.

William spits, and squints against the sparkling sea. A good-size ship ◈ is coming in with the tide. Reckon that's Robert his brother, due with a load of iron.

Robert the sailor's heart always thumps faster as he steers towards the wharf. Approaching from the sea like this, the castle is so beautiful, so grand. Its massive walls striped like an ancient city, with angled towers, and flags streaming from the battlements – with the wild mountains rising clear in the distance. This trip he's got a new crew member, Huw the Welshman. Huw's strong and useful, and at least he speaks some English as well as his jabber of Welsh. Robert has given him leave to go ashore to the alehouse by Castle Ditch ◈. Just til sundown.

Huw the Welshman stares and stares, stacking everything into his memory. He's got no documents, no hidden weapons to rouse the suspicions of the guards at the West Gate. In front of the alehouse he'll just happen to meet a girl with a basket of seven eggs and a man in a green wool cap. But the meeting is vital. Cellars and underground tunnels ◈ run between certain houses here in the town. He needs to know which, and where.

Some Welsh are loyal to the King. Some fight in his armies. But others long to free their country from English rule. King Edward II is facing rebellious barons throughout his lands. Who knows what will happen? Spies need to keep in contact.

High up above the gatehouse, William checks the twelve iron spikes made by Hova the smith to keep the birds from sitting on the head of the King's statue. They're working well. No white streaks stain the King's face. But, on his knee, there's already a splash of bird droppings. William pokes it away.

Hand over hand, William begins climbing down the ladders. Then stops, part way. What if Edward II never comes back? Then the statue carved by him, William the mason, will be the closest the King ever gets to his castle at Caernarfon.

17

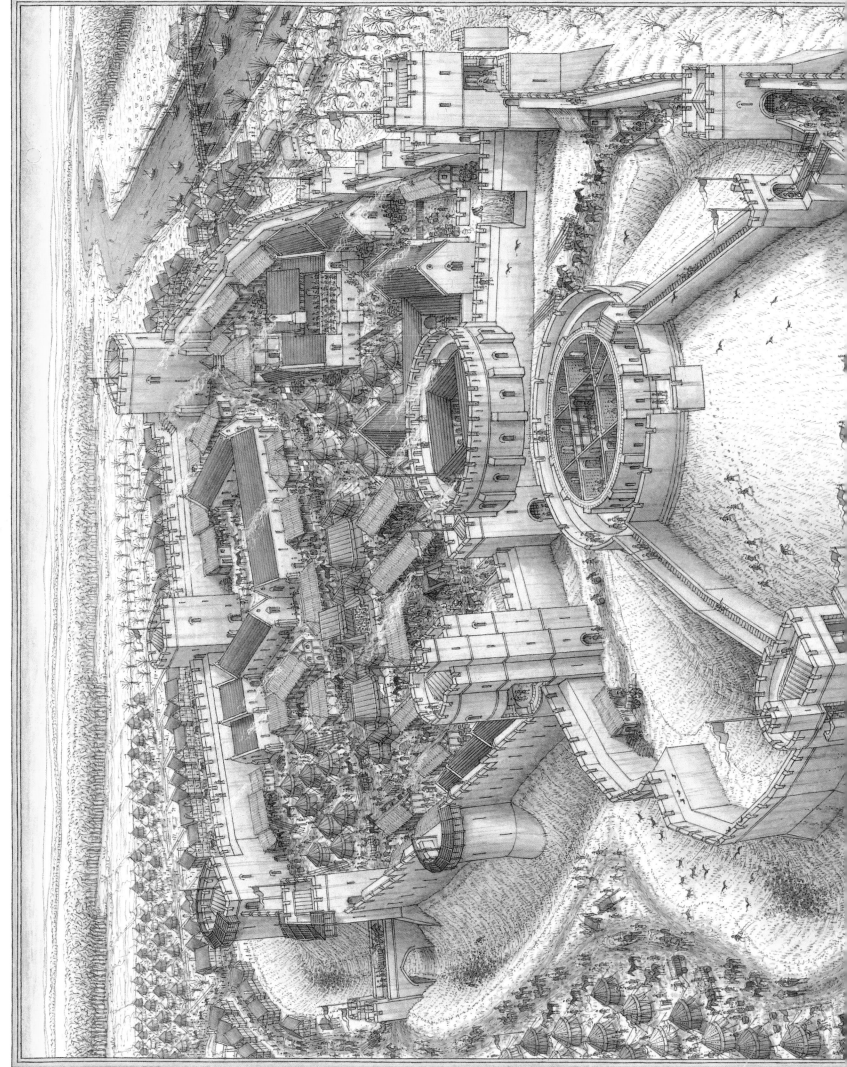

A MAGNIFICENT TOURNAMENT FILLS WINDSOR CASTLE.
Edward III, King of England, has challenged all-comers
with his thirteen-year-old son Edward, Prince of
Wales, and a team of eighteen chosen knights.

The sun hangs low and golden in the sky. ➤

WINDSOR CASTLE
———

JANUARY 19, 1344

The grass crackles with frost. Footprints show green against the white. The vast castle throbs with excitement. Strong, brave men are fighting – fighting to win. Each keys up his nerves, willing himself to perform. Each calls on God and his lady to help him. Each is fighting to prove his courage and prowess.

Horses neigh and stamp. The clear blasts of horns, the jangle of harnesses, the shouts of the crowds – a tournament is always high drama, real danger. And this tournament, held in the royal castle of Windsor, is the best of all.

Henry de Brodeston is helped into the saddle. Strapped inside his armor, he has become a weapon. His servants keep his plate armor bright and polished and his mail coat free of rust, they oil the joints over elbows, knees and armpits. But now he's inside – no one can guess what he's thinking.

Henry remembers what it's like to be knocked off his horse, to thud sprawled on the ground, bruised and bleeding. But the herald is sounding the trumpet, calling him into the lists to joust. He has three runs against his opponent, three chances to unseat him. Men-at-arms stand guard at the strong wooden barriers ◇. Judges watch, ready to call a halt.

Henry grips his lance tightly under his arm. It's split-second timing – spurring his highly trained war horse to full gallop – swerving the horse at the last moment to avoid a head-on collision – keeping his hand and arm at one with the lance, so the blow is struck with maximum power. He can feel his armor against the curved supporting back of the saddle, the trickle of sweat down his spine.

Edward III comes all grimed and flushed to greet his lady, the Queen Philippa. He has just won – again. Philippa is sitting in a specially built stand ◇, accompanied by ladies of the Court. She knows how much Edward wants to re-create the chivalry of the knights of old, and the famous court of the great King Arthur. She has read the stories in her precious books.

Queen Philippa gazes out at the brilliantly decorated castle. Heralds issue challenges, shouting their master's name and rank. Grooms lead the valuable wide-backed war-horses to the stables ◇. Blacksmiths hammer horseshoes, swordsmiths adjust weapons ◇, saddlers stitch last-minute repairs. Minstrels warm their hands in front of braziers. Heaps of glorious food simmer and sizzle in the kitchens ◇. Outside the castle walls, tents have been set up for the overflow of servants and retainers   .

This tournament of Edward's is magical. Yesterday, the first day, there was a grand procession. Knights paraded in painted masks and headdresses, disguised as dragons, wildmen, devils, elephants, lions, peacocks. Afterwards, all the ladies, wearing their most gorgeous clothes, dined together in the great hall ◇. Then the King, lords and knights, who had dined in tents and pavilions ◇8, joined them for dancing and music. Edward has invited the wives of leading citizens to come to the castle as well. Windsor is crammed. Sleep is hardly possible.

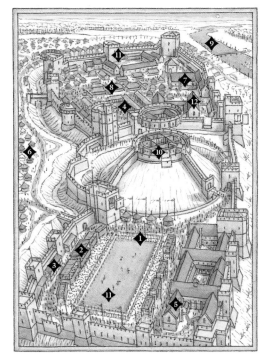

King Edward knows what he is doing. Tournaments are practice for war. Jousts test a man's ability to fight alone. Team events test men's ability to fight together in small groups. At this tournament the young eager squires will be given their chance to joust on the last day. But everyone is hoping for the high risk and danger of a mêlée, when two teams of knights fight in a limited space with prizes, and the chance to capture horses.

The King is young, warlike, ambitious. Everyone admires his royal qualities, his fighting skills. The reign of his father Edward II ended disastrously. But his grandfather was the famous Edward I. Now Edward wants the time of England's glory to come again.

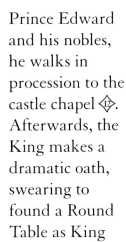

Windsor is Edward's favorite castle. He was born here. Begun by William the Conqueror, the huge castle rising on a ridge by the river Thames ◇9 has a round tower ◇10 on a Norman motte, two vast baileys ◇11, and a great park filled with game for hunting. Edward understands the value of using the castle for royal events.

On the fourth day of the tournament, the King adds to Windsor's importance. An announcement is made. Nobody may leave without permission. Next morning, Thursday, everyone must dress in their best robes.

At the appointed time, King Edward appears richly dressed, wearing his crown. With Queen Philippa, Prince Edward and his nobles, he walks in procession to the castle chapel ◇12. Afterwards, the King makes a dramatic oath, swearing to found a Round Table as King Arthur once did, with 300 knights. Earls, barons and knights swear to support the king. Then everyone joins in a magnificent, happy feast, with more food and wine than anyone can imagine.

But war begins in France. King Edward leads his army to battle. By the time he returns home, his plans to found a Round Table have changed. He creates a new exclusive order of chivalry, the Order of the Garter. The Garter knights are divided into two small groups, like tournament teams, one led by the King, one by the young Prince Edward, now called the Black Prince. Many of the Garter knights are young. Most have fought at the famous battle of Crécy. At Garter ceremonies, they will wear a blue garter above their left knee, embroidered with the motto, 'Evil to him who evil thinks.'

The Garter Knights will need splendid places to feast, to meet, and to pray. King Edward wants a grand royal residence, a great fortified palace suitable for a true warrior king. He starts to rebuild Windsor Castle, the setting for his dreams.

BODIAM CASTLE

— ❦ —

MAY 25, 1392

FIGHTING IN FRANCE HAS MADE SIR EDWARD DALLINGRIDGE A RICH MAN. He builds a fine new castle in the English countryside with his wife, Lady Elizabeth.

Sir Edward rolls out of bed. Careful now, his old wound hurts, especially early in the morning. No nonsense in his castle about toilets – there's one just where he needs it, next to his bed-chamber. His castle has all the latest ideas. Twenty-eight toilets with stone shafts emptying deep into the moat. ➤

A fine well ◇1, right by the kitchen. Thirty-three fireplaces. And it has good defences. Twelve years ago, he was badly wounded when the French attacked a nearby port. Those rogues of Frenchmen won't come raiding up the river to attack him here.

Sir Edward gazes out of the window, sucking a piece of bread dipped in wine. It's his favorite start to the day. His sheep are grazing on the marshes, amongst the wildflowers. Carp rise to snap at mayflies in the moat. He leans further out. Blackhand Seth's in the coracle, working on the toilet outlets as he ordered. The servants keep throwing rubbish down the stone shafts and blocking them. It's the first day of the annual Bodiam Fair, and the sun is shining. Good. That means crowds and healthy profits.

Lady Elizabeth is already in the solar ◇2, giving orders to the butler. The castle is full of guests. Tonight there's a feast, with jugglers and acrobats from the fair entertaining in the great hall ◇3. The servants must watch out for thieves. She can't be everywhere.

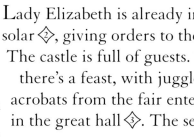

In the kitchen ◇4, everyone grumbles. There's too much to do. The guest of honor, the Abbott, wants a fat swan and it hasn't arrived. Sim the kitchen boy turns the spit filled with roasting fowls. He's already burnt his hand and is crying. Roger the pastry cook has a sore on his leg, and now he's expected to

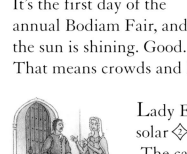

bake five eel pies, five pies with venison and ten with pigeons. Peter the white-food cook has a headache. Listlessly he mixes the minced chicken with cream, rice and almonds. Crash! The dairymaid Joan drops a yellow jug and tosses the pieces into the moat. The new kitchen maid, who's so shy no one knows her name, is up in the tower collecting eggs in the dovecot ◇5. The birds swoop and flap around her head.

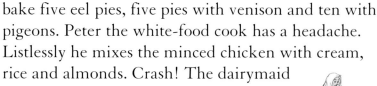

Herbert the page races through the gatehouse ◇6. Nurse pants after him. He's got her precious Pilgrim's Badge, proving she's been all the way to Canterbury on a pilgrimage. Herbert dangles the badge over the edge of the drawbridge. A fat watchman pushes past and treads on his toe. The badge jumps out of his fingers, down into the moat. Herbert likes teasing, he always waits till everyone is especially busy, but he didn't mean to drop Nurse's treasure. Now he'll be beaten and locked up. There'll be no fair, and no feast.

Down at the harbor ◇7 merchants count boxes and bales piled on the wharf. Ships have come up river from the sea, loaded with goods. Sharp German knives, pewter plates and cooking pots, needles, nails, leather gloves and leather buckets, silk ribbons and spices, woodmen's axes, spurs for ladies. Carts and packhorses haul loads up the dusty road to the fair in front of the old manor house. Goods are being laid out on trestles and stalls. People are already trying on, and buying.

Three horsemen ride past the fair and down a track between rows of grapevines. The castle of Bodiam rises in front of them, fortified and strong, surrounded by a wide moat, with ponds and a river winding beyond. To one side are fields and cottages, with a watermill ◈ and the wharf. On the other, marshes stretch towards the distant sea.

The horseman in the lead is a knight, straight from the wars. His padded jacket is stained with rust from his coat of mail. A scar scores his forehead and cheek.

A squire, his son, rides with him. His beard is small and fashionably forked, and his jacket has the latest long, wide sleeves. The third horseman is their servant, his face roughened by wind and sun. He carries a bow and wears a guard on his bow arm, a sword by one side, a dagger on the other. Arrows, feathers smooth and ready for flight, are tucked through his belt.

The horsemen gallop forward, then carefully, warily, approach the castle by the timber bridge ◈ from the moat's edge. Sir Edward watches them keenly from the battlements. At the octagon ◈, they turn at right angles and ride over the next bridge to the barbican tower ◈, then on across the last bridge to the gatehouse. At each point they are challenged. Then they are inside the courtyard. With a shout of joy, Sir Edward runs forward. He hasn't seen his old friend Sir Robert Villars since they fought together in France twenty-five years ago. Lady Elizabeth curtsies to her new guests.

Her niece Alice gazes shyly at the handsome young squire.

Lady Elizabeth sighs. She won't be able to get any sense out of her husband now. She knows him well. They've been married since she was sixteen, and he seventeen. It will be endless soldiers' talk: battles and raids, tournaments and wounds, stories of the old King Edward III and his son Edward the Black Prince, both dead now, bless them. She will have to rearrange the places for the feast. Everyone must sit according to their rank.

25

But, as she goes towards the great hall, two horsemen hurry into the courtyard. A man in a long grey cloak, with cool eyes, accompanied by a man-at-arms. They have ridden for three days with important letters for Sir Edward Dallingridge from the young King, Richard II.

The king's business comes before everything. Sir Edward must leave Bodiam for the Tower of London at first light. But now – there's the feast. And two more guests!

CASTEL SANT'ANGELO

— ❧ —

MAY 6, 1527

ENEMY TROOPS BREAK THROUGH THE WALLS SURROUNDING THE CITY OF ROME, EARLY ON MONDAY MORNING, MAY 6. Just in time, Pope Clement VII flees to the great fortress of Castel Sant'Angelo.

The crush of frantic, sweating people is frightful. Everyone is trying to escape from the advancing soldiers. Benvenuto Cellini knows what's happening.

At first light, he went out to the city walls and saw the swarming army beyond, ➤

saw their grappling ladders, the bodies of dead defenders sprawled on the ramparts. He heard the shrieks, the crack of gunshot.

Since midnight, the great bell of the Capitol has been tolling, calling the city's defenders to their posts. Terror spreads through Rome's narrow streets, its hostels for pilgrims, its nunneries, shops and palaces.

Benvenuto is young and strong. He barges through the crowds towards the bulk of Castel Sant'Angelo, crouching brown-grey above the River Tiber. Rome's ancient fortress, its secretive prison, its palace and refuge for the Popes. He arrives just as the drawbridge ◇ over the moat is being raised, and manages to get inside. Behind him, desperate people are shoved forward and tumble into the moat. An officer grabs him. "To the battlements! To the guns!"

Up on the battlements ◇2, all is confusion. The Commander of the gunners weeps uncontrollably. He can see his house being robbed, his wife and children attacked. Along the river's edge ◇3, families throw possessions into overloaded boats. Benvenuto grabs a burning fuse, aims a cannon, steadies his nerve. And shoots.

Pope Clement VII and his Cardinals run along a secret corridor ◇4 above the battle raging in the streets below, fleeing from the Vatican to Castel Sant'Angelo. A Cardinal is hauled inside the fortress in a basket ◇5,

another is pushed through a window ◇6. Three manage to scrabble up the walls.

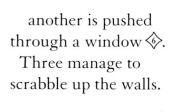

No one knows all the secrets of Castel Sant'Angelo. Fourteen hundred years ago, the Emperor Hadrian built a great drum-shaped monument here to hold his ashes. The Roman Emperor's monument is still the core of the building. But now it is riddled with hidden passages ◇7, private stairs, dreadful dungeons. Apartments have been built at the top for the Pope ◇8, with elegant reception rooms and a little decorated bathroom.

There's not enough food, or water, for the 950 civilians and soldiers crammed inside Castel Sant' Angelo. Outside, the invading troops ◇9 of the Emperor Charles V begin to dig in for a siege, cutting the castle off.

Benvenuto is given command of five guns at the top of the keep, under the statue of the angel ◇10. He primes his weapons and repairs them when they get damaged. Before the attack on Rome, Benvenuto Cellini was a successful goldsmith, making beautiful jewellery and ornaments for rich clients. But he loves to fight. He's 27 years old, proud of his skill as a gunner. Every day he kills some of the enemy.

The great city of Rome is being sacked by out-of-control soldiers who loot, rampage and murder. The smell of gunshot and burning fills the air, mixing with the stench of open drains and decaying bodies. The horrors of plague and famine infect the city.

28

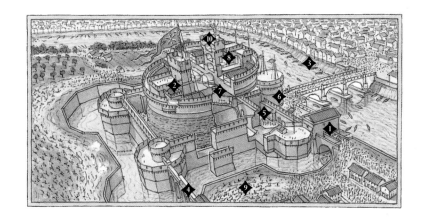

Benvenuto is summoned to a small, locked room in the castle. Inside, he finds Pope Clement VII with one trusted servant, and all the glittering treasures of the Papal regalia. The Pope needs gold to help pay off the enemy. Benvenuto is ordered to remove the jewels from their settings,

and secretly melt down the gold. Carefully, he takes the diamonds and emeralds, the big blue sapphires, red rubies and glowing pearls, wrapping each precious gem in a bit of paper, and sewing it into the clothes of the Pope and his servant. Then he climbs to his room at the top of the keep and builds a little furnace. While the gold melts, he watches for any chance to use his guns, running from the heat of the furnace to the din and smell of his cannon.

In a few days, Castel Sant'Angelo surrenders, and Benvenuto leaves with the garrison.

Ten years later, Benvenuto Cellini is back inside Castel Sant'Angelo. This time he is a prisoner. His enemies accuse him of keeping some of the Papal jewels during the Sack of Rome. Pope Clement VII, who knew he was innocent, is dead. The new Pope keeps him in prison.

But Benvenuto escapes. He cuts some linen sheets into strips and sews them together to make ropes. He pulls the nails out of the hinges in his door and covers the gaps with false nail heads made of wax and rust. One night, he manages to get his prison door open, climb out the lavatory window of the keep, lower himself down by his sheeting rope, swarm up the next wall using a long pole, climb down the other side with another sheeting rope, then, exhausted, with bleeding hands, use the last of his ropes to get

over the third wall. Near the bottom, he falls, hurts his head, and breaks his leg. He binds up his leg, crawls to the city gate, is attacked by a dog, and saved by a Cardinal who gets a doctor to set his leg. At least – this is how Benvenuto tells the story.

But the Pope imprisons him again in Castel Sant'Angelo. This time, Benvenuto is locked in a dreadful, gloomy dungeon, infested with spiders and worms. The wet floor rots his mattress. Sick and weak, Benvenuto fears he will never be freed. He longs to feel the warmth of the sun, just once, before he dies.

Benvenuto Cellini is hot-tempered, a brave fighter, who says what he thinks. And he is such a superb artist that Francis I, King of France, wants him to be his goldsmith. With the King's help Benvenuto is finally released from Castel Sant' Angelo. That brooding fortress by the River Tiber, that place of grandeur and suffering, of power and the abuse of power.

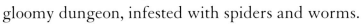

TOWER OF LONDON

—⚶⚶—

MAY 29, 1533

**KING HENRY VIII OF ENGLAND WAITS
IMPATIENTLY AT THE TOWER OF LONDON.**
His new Queen, Anne Boleyn, is coming
up the river Thames in a grand coronation
procession.

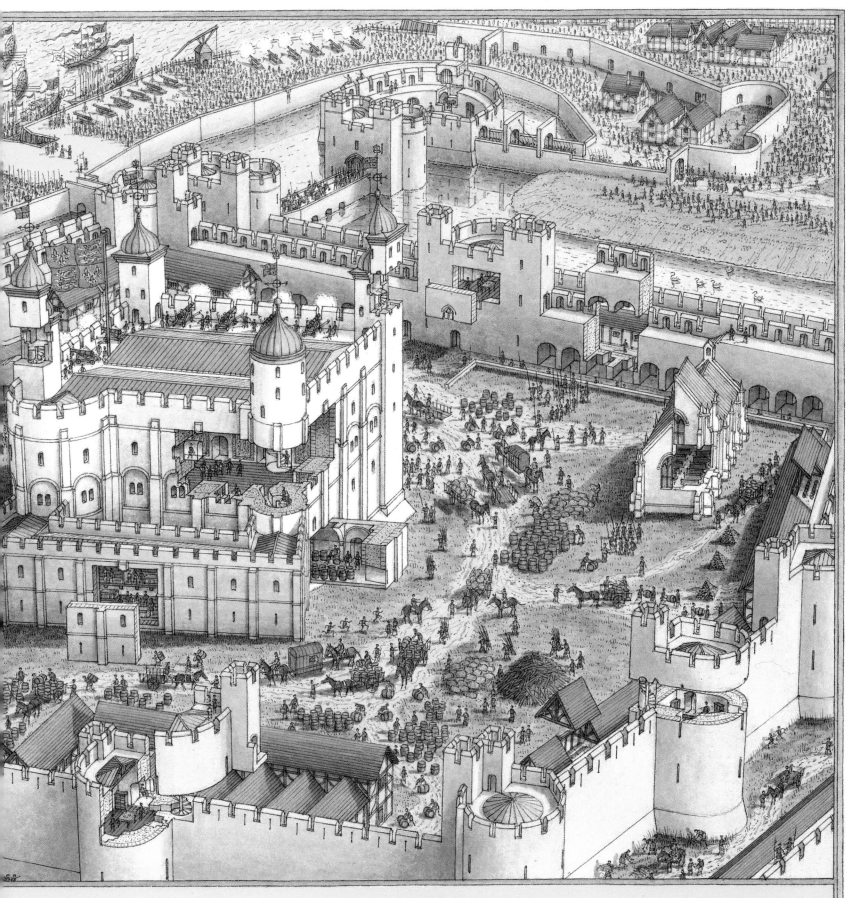

Pickpockets dart amongst the tightly packed crowd. Stall keepers flap flies off pies and trays of sugary cakes. Bored children squabble. Suddenly, the procession appears, moving fast with the tide.

Cannons in the Tower of London boom out. Guns on the ships moored on both shores crack and thunder. ⟶

Fifty decorated barges fill the river, all hung with bright silks, tapestries and banners. Musicians play, the crowds cheer. Here comes the Lord Mayor in his gilded barge ◇, rowed by watermen wearing his livery. And here's the Batchelors' barge ◇, hung with cloth of gold, purple and crimson silks, and flags edged with tinkling bells. Bright-painted shields line the barge's sides. Banners of beaten metal gleam in the afternoon sun.

A gunboat appears, with a dragon surrounded by yelling monsters and wild men. The dragon's tail thrashes, and fire spits from its jaws. The crowd gasps. There's a second gunboat with a white falcon wearing a crown and the words in gold, "Happiest of Women." And at last comes the happiest woman, the Queen, dressed in gold.

Anne steps from her barge and walks to where King Henry VIII stands, big, bold, confident, by the main gatehouse of the Tower ◇. Henry kisses his new Queen. He is giving her a magnificent coronation, beginning at the Tower of London. England's monarchs always stay here at the Tower before being crowned.

Henry and Anne go inside to newly decorated apartments ◇ in the royal palace. That evening, a banquet is held in the great hall ◇. All night, music is played and fireworks

bang and crackle along the river, with rounds of celebratory gunfire from the Tower. In the Royal Menagerie ◇, the lions in their cages roar mournfully.

The Tower dominates Londoners. High grey walls and strong gates, wide moat and jumble of buildings, the Tower of London has grown over five centuries around William the Conqueror's great Norman castle ◇. It stands for the power and splendor of England's monarchs. The nation's weapons are stored inside. So are the royal treasure, and official documents. Kings have been besieged here, taken prisoner, deposed. Prisoners enter its gates in fear and despair.

On Saturday, May 31, Anne leaves the Tower ◇ and begins her procession through London to Westminster Abbey and her coronation. Gravel covers the streets to stop the horses from slipping.

Constables dressed in velvet and silk, holding great staves, line the route keeping the crowd behind barriers. Anne is dressed in silver. She sits proudly on a litter of cloth of gold, pulled by two palfreys covered in white damask. Four knights hold a golden canopy over her.

Londoners don't like Anne. The streets are hung with silks and carpets, and banners with the letters HA for Henry and Anne. Ha! Ha! – shout the crowds. But Anne, high-spirited, stylish, sharp-tongued, smiles, and admires all the pageants, shows and triumphal arches along the way.

For six years, Henry has wooed Anne. Month after month, she resisted the

32

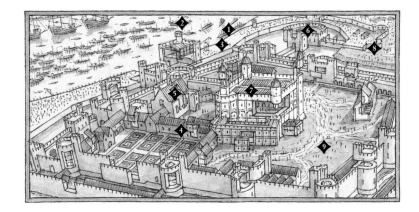

demands of a powerful King, used to getting what he wanted. Henry is tired of his old Queen, Catherine. Only one of her five pregnancies has resulted in a living child, a girl, and now she can have no more. Henry needs a son to inherit the throne. He is passionately in love with his darling Anne and wants to marry her. Pope Clement VII in Rome won't give him permission to divorce Catherine.

But, this January, Henry married Anne, secretly. Now he has ignored the Pope and had himself declared divorced. Anne is already pregnant, and astrologers, wizards and doctors all predict it's a boy.

Henry cannot wait for his son to be born. Early in September, Queen Anne gives birth to a healthy baby. But it's a girl, called Elizabeth.

Elizabeth is just over two and a half when Anne her mother goes back to the Tower of London. This time, the Queen is rowed in a barge with no ceremony. "Shall I go into a dungeon?" she asks the governor of the Tower. "No, Madam, you shall go into your lodging that you lay in at your coronation," he replies. Anne kneels, and weeps. Terrible charges have been brought against her, her brother and other men at Court. They are tried in the great hall. Anne denies everything, but she is found guilty of high treason and condemned to death, as the King has planned. Henry now hates her. He has fallen in love again and wants to remarry. After two more pregnancies, Anne has failed to give him a living son.

In the royal apartments, Anne is never left alone. People listen at the doors, report everything she says. Her brother and the other accused men are executed, and the scaffold is built for her in the open space on the north side of the Tower ◈. Anne complains about the noise of hammering. It is the night before her death.

On the morning of May 19, 1536, Anne, dressed in grey, is led to the scaffold. The twenty people witnessing the execution listen to her last words. Then she takes off her white collar, and her hood embroidered with pearls, and kneels. An expert headsman has come from France to use a sword, not an axe. Anne is the first English queen ever to be beheaded.

With a single stroke, Anne is dead. Her life as Henry's crowned Queen began in the Tower of London almost exactly three years ago. And now it ends here, a small head rolling away from its body.

CHAMBORD
—⋇—
DECEMBER 18, 1539

THE DAY'S HUNTING HAS JUST ENDED. Francis I, King of France, is entertaining his guest, the Emperor Charles V at his Chateau of Chambord.

Guy's hounds tug at their leashes. Briff, Guy's favorite, lifts a torn paw and whines. Huntsmen, dressed in winter grey, gallop past. Grooms run, orders are shouted. Up on Chambord's roof, courtiers and ladies crowd the terraces to watch the returning hunt.

Today was his best day ever, Guy decides. He's been out since frosty dawn, hunting amongst the ancient oaks, ➡

the marshes and still pools of the Royal Forest ◇. Guy lives for hunting. He loves the fresh air and hard exercise, the sound of the horns calling through the trees. Ever since he was apprenticed to a master hunter at age seven, he's been learning the skills. Now he's twenty, he's got three horses and his own hounds.

He's a true hunter at last.

The vast castle of Chambord, with its fairytale turrets and towers, seems to float in the cold air above the water of the moat ◇. Magical, like a dream. Yet twelve thousand people are here – or eighteen thousand. Who knows the exact number? They've all suddenly arrived at this lonely place in the middle of the forest, needing food and somewhere to sleep. All gossiping and scheming and competing for attention. They've come because King Francis I is entertaining the Emperor Charles V as magnificently as he possibly can. This is the Emperor's first visit to France. He's passing through, travelling from Spain north to the Netherlands.

Years ago, after a battle, King Francis was captured and kept by the Emperor in a Spanish prison, the worst humiliation in his whole life. King Francis and the Emperor are regularly at war with each other. They are rivals. Yet – here they are at Chambord, being friends!

But Guy knows what people are whispering. The Emperor is nervous and wary. Two nights ago, at another chateau, he was nearly stifled by smoke and trampled in the panic after a page dropped a torch and a tapestry went up in flames. No one wants any accidents here at Chambord.

To Guy, it all seems a huge expensive piece of play-acting. Not like today in the forest. That was real. Today he had the honor of showing the Emperor where a mighty stag had pushed through dense scrub, bending branches and snapping twigs with his great antlers. He watched the King's falcon fighting a kestrel, the two birds tumbling and veering high in the pale sky. And he saw a massive wild boar killed in his den. That was almost too real! The valiant boar charged a horse. Would have ripped it with his tusks if Count Gaston hadn't thrust down with his spear just in time.

Briff whimpers. Guy has jobs to do. He must take care of his horses. The hounds must be seen to – they'll need a fire tonight in the kennels, it's so cold. Briff's sore feet must be washed in sheep's tallow boiled with wine. When his jobs are done, Guy can join the master hunter in a drink, eat his dinner, and unroll his mattress for a well-earned sleep.

Winter after winter, summer after summer, the vast castle of Chambord is silent and deserted. The hundreds of rooms closed up, empty. Cold stone walls. Bare floors. Unlit fires. No one walking up the famous double spiral staircase ◈. No one wandering amongst the carved stone chimneys ◈ on the roof.

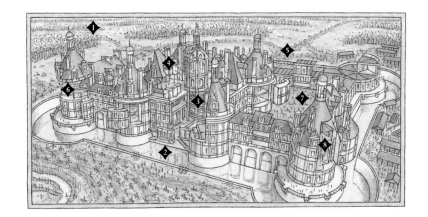

Then – suddenly – King Francis decides to visit, and Chambord buzzes with frenzied activity. Thousands of servants rush ahead of the King. Hundreds of waggons and carts ◈, piled with furniture, creak through fields and woodlands. Everything Francis needs travels with him as he moves around his kingdom. Best beds are unpacked and hauled upstairs into bed chambers ◈, trestle tables assembled in the dining halls,

chandeliers hung from hooks, pots and pans piled into the kitchens. Vast amounts of food must be found in surrounding villages and towns, barrels of wine and beer, barn-fulls of fodder for the horses ◈, great heaps of wood for cooking.

Where the King goes, the Court follows. Rooms heave with hopeful hangers-on, desperate askers-of-favors, artists, doctors, courtiers and nobles. Crowds of officials carry out government business, bishops and lawyers hover, army commanders strut. And everywhere there are the King's special pleasure – beautiful ladies.

But this December at Chambord, Francis wants to dazzle the Emperor. Stone walls disappear behind glowing velvet hangings   embroidered with flowers and animals. There are hangings of shimmering taffeta, and rich damasks crusted with jewels. Cloths of silver and gold drape the ceilings. Candles blaze in gold and silver candelabra. Golden plates glitter

on sideboards. Gorgeous canopies of embroidered silk and satin hang over beds, loop above chairs. Each room is like a brilliant jewel box, competing with the next.

King Francis is tall and dark-haired, handsome and regal. He's proud of his slim legs. Tonight he wears the latest fashion, exquisite satin slashed with silk, embroidered with pearls. Francis loves hard physical exercise, hunting, fighting and dancing. He surrounds himself with artists, books, good conversation. Sadly he has not been feeling well. But tonight, a feast has been arranged with at least thirty courses. It's all part of the show. Emperors and Kings believe they must appear wealthy beyond imagining. They must wear the richest clothing and sit down to overwhelming amounts of food.

Francis became King at the age of twenty. Ever since, he has competed with his two greatest rivals, King Henry VIII of England, and the Emperor Charles V. Now, the Emperor's visit gives him the chance to show how powerful and rich he is, what a mighty hunter, what a lover of beautiful women and elegant things. Magnificent Chambord, created by Francis as his hunting lodge in the forest, is his proof.

37

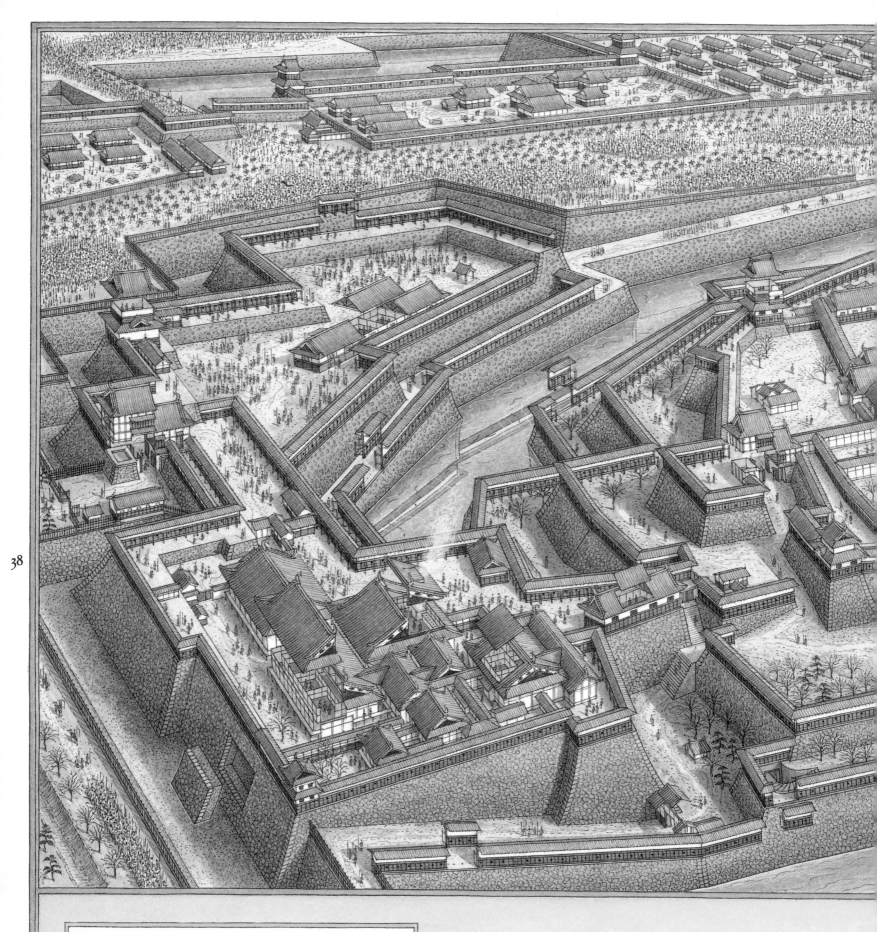

38

OSAKA CASTLE

— ✤ —

NOVEMBER 30, 1614

OSAKA CASTLE PREPARES FOR WAR. Two powerful families, the Toyotomi and the Tokugawa, are locked in conflict. The last battles are about to begin.

A famous warrior gallops up to Osaka Castle with

a hundred picked samurai. They have come to fight for the young Lord Hideyori, leader of the House of Toyotomi. Every day, samurai have been pouring into the castle from all over Japan. The warlords they have fought for are defeated, without land. Now, poor, desperate, with nothing to lose, the samurai will fight for Hideyori. ➤

and arrows, corridors to protect sharp-shooters, holes for hurling down stones, look-out towers, and secret escape routes ◇.

Osaka Castle can withstand a long siege. Its storehouses ◇ are filled with rice and salt. Gold coins are piled in the vaults ◇ of the keep. The gun racks are lined with muskets, there's gunpowder and lead shot, spears, bows and arrows.

Osaka Castle is immensely strong, famous and beautiful – a vast fortress, defended by a deep broad moat ◇, with a second beyond ◇, and a third outer ring of water. Massive stone ramparts ◇ soar 120 feet high. Inside the castle there are barracks ◇ for soldiers, and storehouses for food and weapons. Cool gardens ◇ shade an elegant palace ◇. The walls of the reception chambers ◇ are lined with hammered gold and silver, and beautiful paintings. An imposing black and white eight-storey keep   , decorated with glowing gold, rises next to the palace.

The castle has cunning traps and secret tricks to repel invaders. There are only two entrances. One is over an easily dismantled wooden bridge ◇ across a moat, the other through a small gate ◇. Once inside, paths lead like a confusing maze. Attackers have great difficulty getting in – or once in, out again. They are funnelled towards barriers and dead ends, around sharp corners and U-turns, through low-ceilinged rooms and along meandering passages, past curving walls, up narrow stairs overlooked by parapets where hidden defenders can fire down. There are loop-holes for guns

Osaka Castle was built by Hideyori's father, the great warrior Toyotomi Hideyoshi. After generations of bloody fighting between warring lords, Hideyoshi brought all Japan under his military control. Born the son of a humble foot-soldier, Hideyoshi had an army of a quarter of a million men by the time he built the great fortress of Osaka.

.

Hideyori was still a small child when his father Hideyoshi died. Five guardians swore to Hideyoshi to protect his little son and the rights of the House of Toyotomi. The leader of the guardians was Hideyoshi's second-in-command, Tokugawa Ieyasu. But Ieyasu seized power for himself and the House of Tokugawa.

Hideyori was born in Osaka Castle. He has grown up there, safely, with his mother. But now, aged 22, he is a threat Ieyasu cannot tolerate. Ieyasu summons his armies against Hideyori, his Castle of Osaka, and the supporters of the House of Toyotomi. It will be a fight to the finish between the two families.

The Lord Hideyoshi mixed the ingredients for a cake, people say. But the Lord Ieyasu plans to eat it.

Ieyasu attacks Osaka Castle in December. His vast army is well equipped with muskets, and five cannon purchased from English traders. He and his sons, dressed in splendid armor and mounted on

fine horses, are surrounded by their guards. Formations of samurai line up behind tall banners announcing the names of their lords.

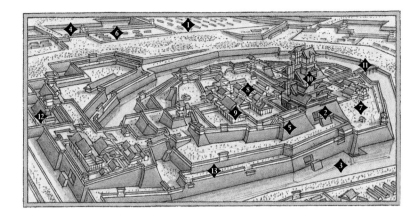

But Ieyasu cannot break through Osaka's magnificent defences. He starts negotiating a truce. Hideyori's mother inside Osaka Castle is eager to agree to terms. Ieyasu orders his cannons to be trained on her distant apartments, and one shot lobs in. Peace is agreed, with an especially solemn and binding document, signed with a "blood stamp," a drop of blood from Ieyasu's finger, under his name.

Ieyasu has suggested that the castle's outer moat and defensive rampart should be filled in, as a sign of good faith. They aren't needed now the war is over. The morning after the peace document is exchanged, Ieyasu's soldiers start work, so fast that the people inside the castle hardly know what is happening. Then the labor squads move forward and begin fill-ing in the second moat. This was never agreed to. Hideyori's commanders protest furiously, and rush to complain. A high official says the extra filling in should not be happening. By the time he arrives to stop the work, the moat is filled. How foolish and careless, the official says. But it's too late for regrets. In any case, with peace there's no need for moats.

Ieyasu attacks again on June 3, 1615. He is 73 years old, and this is his ninetieth battle. Now the two rings of moats are filled, Osaka Castle is vulnerable and Hideyori's soldiers have to fight in the open. Ieyasu's huge army is much bigger than Hideyori's, but the fighting is hard and bloody. Samurai on horseback, foot soldiers armed with lances and swords, struggle, then break away in defeat.

The heads of the fallen are struck off and piled up for a count of the dead.

Hideyori waits inside the gates with his household troops for the signal to ride out and attack. The terrible sounds of battle surround the castle. In the town, the merchants' houses are burning, people fleeing in panic. Acrid smoke from gunfire hangs low, hiding what is happening. All is confusion.

The great keep of the castle is on fire. Sparks and flames spread fast. Enemy troops get through the second line of defence. Hideyori and his mother take refuge in a fireproof storehouse. Next morning, defeat certain, they commit suicide.

Osaka Castle is destroyed. The House of Toyotomi is wiped out. Osaka city, once home to 200,000 people, is a pile of ash and rubble. Ieyasu's sons rebuild Osaka Castle and the city.

For the next 250 years, the House of Tokugawa governs Japan.

42

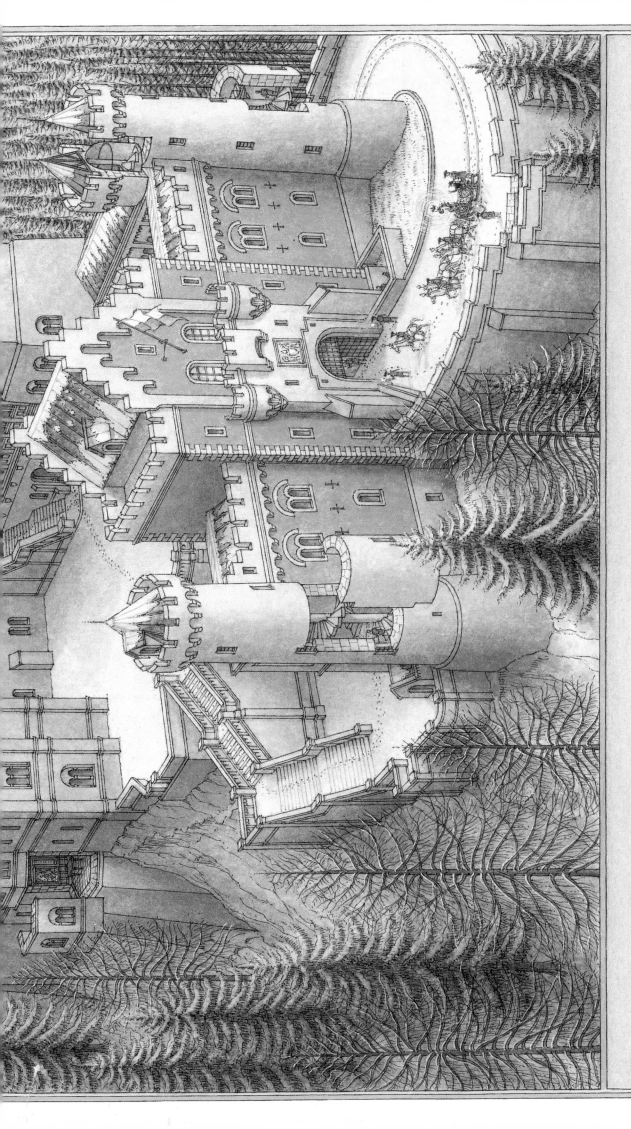

Neuschwanstein

—❧—

February 7, 1886

King Ludwig II of Bavaria is dreaming about his fairytale castle of Neuschwanstein. Tonight he will ride there through the mountains in his sleigh.

Snow creaks under King Ludwig's shoes. The smooth, white crust sparkles like tiny diamonds. ➤

43

The lights of Linderhof Palace spill out into the darkness behind him as he walks up the hill. But the King is thinking about his secret cave, just ahead. Soon he will be inside, gliding across a small lake in a golden boat shaped like a shell, swans drifting beside him.

Inside the artificial cave, an electrician and seven boilermen are hard at work, firing up the generators of Bavaria's first power station. Twenty-four electric lamps begin playing Ludwig's favorite colors of red, pink, blue and green across glittering stalactites. Servants turn on the wave machine and the lake's surface begins to ripple. Stoves hidden inside stalagmites warm the air. None of the mechanisms show! Everything seems magic.

Every day for King Ludwig II of Bavaria begins whenever possible after dark. If he sleeps all day, he can be the Night King. Now, after the cave, he walks back to have dinner in his exquisite small palace of Linderhof. Inside, candlelight flickers and glows in gilded mirrors, on carved wood and painted ceilings. At Linderhof, Ludwig has recreated the world of two hundred years ago, when his favorite King, Louis XIV, ruled France.

Creating fantastic, beautiful buildings is Ludwig's passion. Inside them, he can be in a fantasy-world, cut off from the real world. Deeply shy, Ludwig would rather avoid people. He does not like having to deal with ordinary affairs. He thinks the century he lives in is disgusting and dismal.

Ludwig became King of Bavaria when he was eighteen, and began building almost immediately. Lonely, often un-happy, he builds buildings for him-self, as places where he can escape into his private worlds. Sometimes he dreams on the fabulous peacock throne in the red and purple splendor of his Moorish Pavilion. Sometimes he pretends to be a hero from the old German stories, and stays in a lonely mountain valley where a great tree grows through the floor of a rugged hut, with a sword that cannot be pulled out thrust deep in its trunk.

Sitting alone in his beautiful dining room, Ludwig signals, and his table sinks down through the floor. Below, in the kitchen, his chef has made dinner for four. Heaving and straining, out of sight, servants crank the table back up, up. And it appears – a magic dinner table, with food all ready.

Ludwig sits at the table. His teeth hurt so much, he can only eat soft food. When he came to the throne he was handsome and slim. Now aged 40, his six-feet-four-inch height has thickened and become fat. Sometimes Ludwig has conversations with an imaginary King Louis XIV and other guests. Tonight he eats in silence. The full moon will have risen and he has planned a sleigh ride.

Six white horses are waiting in front of the palace. A carved crown hangs high at the front of the sleigh with an electric light hidden inside. The batteries are in a box by Ludwig's fur-wrapped feet.

Then they are off, through the trees, down the curving drive, out onto the road and up through the mountains. The stillness of night. The privacy. Just the King, riding in his sleigh, and his grooms. Silence, except for the swish of the runners, the panting of the horses. Exhilarating speed. The moonlight steady, white, the shadows flat, almost blue. Up past a lake, reeds standing stiffly in its frozen shallows, and into the long

winding pass.

Between bare cliffs, the stream still runs under the ice. Mountain peaks rise, mysterious, untouchable. Ludwig's cheeks glow with cold. Alone in his beloved Alps, he feels free. Happy.

The sleigh starts down the far side of the pass. Tall pines close darkly around the road. It's deep, deep night. Then they are climbing again, up a winding steep road, through the woods. And there. Romantic, fantastic, poised like a great bird on top of its narrow crag, above a steep wild gorge ◇1, is his beautiful dream castle of Neuschwanstein. Planned by him in every detail. Built as the German knights would have built, six centuries ago. Light pours from the great Singers' Hall ◇2 at the top of the castle. Hundreds of candles in gilded chandeliers and candelabra, all lit, for him alone.

For seventeen years, teams of workmen and craftsmen have been building Neuschwanstein. It isn't finished. That causes Ludwig terrible pain. He has used up all his money and is deeply in debt. But building must go on. If he isn't building, creating beauty, he does not know what to do, and his life is not worth living. The Knights' House ◇3 isn't complete, the guest wing ◇4 next to the ravine is hardly started. The interior of the second floor is an empty shell. There's scaffolding, winches, and piles of stones.

But the Singers' Hall, with its paintings of heroes from German stories, is finished. His Throne Room ◇5, sitting room ◇6, and dining room ◇7, the paintings and wood carvings, the sumptuous silks and brocades, his ingeniously designed central heating and electric lighting, his bedroom ◇8 with the

silver swan giving water through its beak into a silver basin, and the kitchen with its latest technology – they all are finished. Now he can live in Neuschwanstein. And his castle is utterly, totally private. Not for people to stare at.

Ludwig gazes from the sleigh   . In his mind, he can hear music pouring from the Singers' Hall, the music of his friend the composer Richard Wagner. Ludwig knows exactly what his beautiful castle should look like. And this is how he sees it, rising majestic, magically complete, in the moonlight.

In four months, King Ludwig is dead. Declared insane, and removed from the throne by his government, he drowns in a lake with his doctor. No one knows how it happened.

I want to be a mystery, Ludwig once wrote, to myself, and to everyone else.

45

GLOSSARY

Baggage train ~ a line of baggage-animals carrying an army's equipment

Bailey ~ the outer wall of a castle, often surrounding a motte

Barbican tower ~ a watchtower over a castle gate

Barge ~ a kind of boat

Blockade ~ cutting off a place by surrounding it

Brazier ~ a container for hot coals

Butler ~ a male servant

Capitol ~ a temple in Rome

Cardinal ~ an important official in the Catholic Church

Cavalry ~ soldiers on horseback

Chivalry ~ a system of knighthood, associated with bravery and courtesy

Cistern ~ a water tank

Coracle ~ a small oval rowing boat

Crusade ~ an expedition in medieval times to conquer the Holy Land

Curfew ~ a regulation obliging people to be indoors by a certain time, often signalled by the ringing of a bell

Curtain wall ~ a wall which does not support a roof

Damask ~ a rich material woven with a pattern

Deposed ~ removed from a position of power

Detachment ~ a group of soldiers away from the main army

Fodder ~ food for animals

Fortification ~ a construction to help defend a military position

Game ~ meat from animals hunted for sport

Gangrene ~ decay of part of the body

Garrison ~ a group of soldiers stationed in a town or fortress

Glazier ~ someone who sets glass in window-frames

Headsman ~ an executioner who cuts off heads

Herald ~ someone who makes announcements

Holy Land ~ parts of the Middle East where events described in the Bible took place

Islam ~ the Muslim religion

Joust ~ a contest between two knights on horseback carrying lances

Keep ~ the central tower of a castle

Lance ~ a weapon for use on horseback with a long shaft and a spearhead

Lists ~ the place where jousting takes place

Litter ~ a couch carried by men or animals

Livery ~ the special dress of a person's servants

Man-at-arms ~ a soldier

Mason ~ someone who works with stone

Mêlée ~ a noisy fight

Menagerie ~ a zoo

Minstrel ~ a musician

Motte ~ a mound with a castle keep, often surrounded by a bailey

Musket ~ a type of large gun

Naphtha ~ a kind of oil which can be set alight

Page ~ a boy training to be a knight

Palfrey ~ a horse for a lady

Papal ~ to do with a pope

Pewter ~ a type of metal

Pilgrimage ~ a journey to a holy place

Pope ~ the head of the Roman Catholic Church

Rampart ~ a flat-topped defensive mound or wall

Regalia ~ a powerful person's special clothes or jewels

Reinforcement ~ extra troops

Retainer ~ a personal attendant in a noble household

Ricochet ~ to bounce off

Samurai ~ a Japanese soldier

Sapper ~ a soldier who undermines enemy positions

Scaffold ~ a raised platform for executions

Sentinel ~ a guard

Siege ~ surrounding a castle, or cutting off its supplies and attacking it to make it surrender

Solar ~ an upper room

Stockade ~ a barrier made of wooden stakes

Stocks ~ a wooden punishment device which holds a person by the ankles and sometimes wrists

Taffeta ~ a thin, glossy silk material

Tavern ~ an inn

Tournament ~ a sport in which players take part on horseback e.g. jousting

Treason ~ disloyalty to the ruler or government

Treaty ~ a formal agreement

Truce ~ a suspension of war

Vatican ~ where the Pope lives in Rome

Venison ~ meat from deer

Ward (inner, middle) ~ a courtyard of a castle

Waterman ~ a ferryman

Wharf ~ the bank of a river where boats land

INDEX OF PEOPLE & PLACES

All the people named below really existed.

Arthur, King 20-21

Baybars, Sultan of Egypt 10-13

Bodiam 22-25

Bogis 9

Boleyn, Anne 30-33

Caernarfon 14-17

Castel Sant'Angelo 26-29

Catherine, Queen of England 33

Cellini, Benvenuto 26-29

Chambord 34-37

Chateau Gaillard 6-9

Charles V, Emperor 28, 34-37

Clement VII, Pope 26-29, 33

Dallingridge, Lady Elizabeth 22-25

Dallingridge, Sir Edward 22-25

Edward I, King of England 13-14, 16, 21

Edward II, King of England 16-17

Edward III, King of England 19-21, 25

Edward, Prince of Wales 19, 21, 25

Eleanor, Queen 16

Elizabeth, Princess 33

Francis I, King of France 29, 34-37

Gaillard, Chateau 6-9

Hadrian, Emperor 28

Henry VIII, King of England 30-33, 37

John, King of England 9

Knights of St. John 10-13

Krak des Chevaliers 10-13

Linderhof 44

Louis XIV, King of France 44

Ludwig II, King of Bavaria 43-45

Neuschwanstein 42-45

Osaka 38-41

Philip Augustus, King of France 8-9

Philippa, Queen 20-21

Richard I, King of England 7-9

Richard II, King of England 25

Saladin 8

Thames, River 21, 31-32

Tiber, River 28-29

Tokugawa Ieyasu 40-41

Tower of London 25, 30-33

Toyotomi Hideyori 38-41

Toyotomi Hideyoshi 40

William the Conqueror 21, 32

Windsor 18-21

47

First American Edition published in 2004 by
Enchanted Lion Books, 115 West 18 Street, New York, NY 10011

Consultant: Christopher Gravett

Picture research by ProudSmith Publishing Services.

Design by Gill Willis.

Library of Congress Catalog-in-Publishing Data
Hooper, Meredith.
Stephen Biesty's Castles / written by Meredith Hooper. —1st American ed.
p. cm.
Illustrated by Stephen Biesty.
Includes index.
ISBN 1-59270-031-4
1. Castles. 2. Civilization, Medieval. I. Title: Castles. II.
Biesty, Stephen. III. Title..
GT3350 .H66
940.1—dc22   2003071047

Printed in China by WKT.
Color reproduction by Dt Gradations Ltd, UK